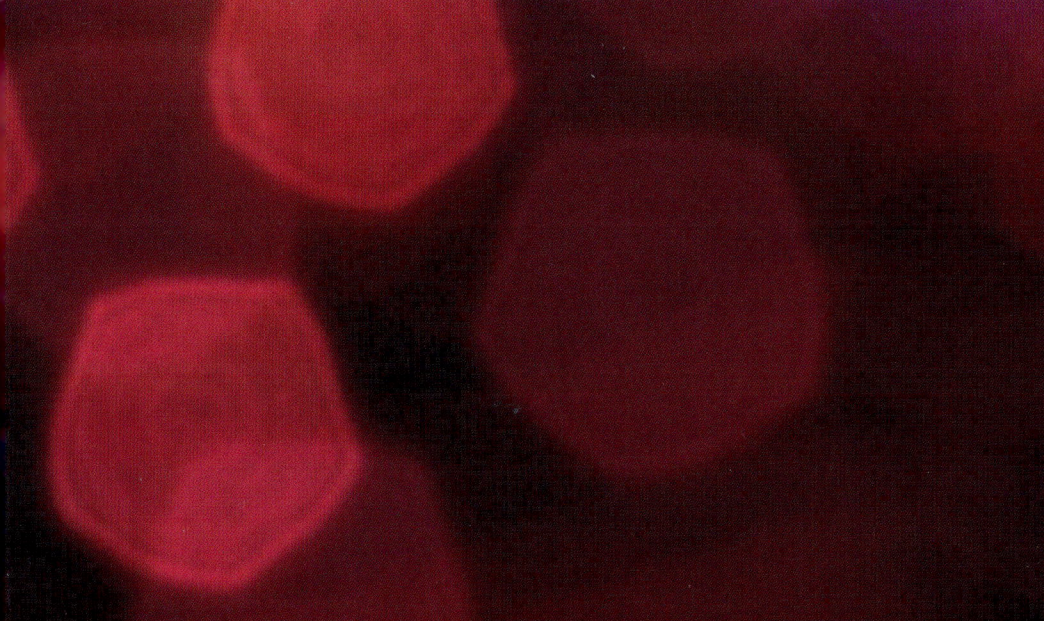

CONTEMPORARY LIVES

NICKI MINAJ

RAPPER & FASHION STAR

ABDO
Publishing Company

NICKI MINAJ

RAPPER & FASHION STAR

by Ashley Rae Harris

CREDITS

Published by ABDO Publishing Company, PO Box 398166, Minneapolis, MN 55439. Copyright © 2013 by Abdo Consulting Group, Inc. International copyrights reserved in all countries. No part of this book may be reproduced in any form without written permission from the publisher. The Essential Library™ is a trademark and logo of ABDO Publishing Company.

Printed in the United States of America,
North Mankato, Minnesota
092012
012013

 THIS BOOK CONTAINS AT LEAST 10% RECYCLED MATERIALS.

Editor: Megan Anderson
Series Designer: Emily Love

Cataloging-in-Publication Data

Harris, Ashley Rae.
 Nicki Minaj: rapper & fashion star / Ashley Rae Harris.
   p. cm. -- (Contemporary lives)
Includes bibliographical references and index.
ISBN 978-1-61783-622-0
1. Minaj, Nicki, 1982- --Juvenile literature. 2. Rap musicians--United States--Biography--Juvenile literature. 3. Hip-hop--United States--Biography--Juvenile literature. 1. Title.
782.421649092--dc15
[B]

2012945987

TABLE OF CONTENTS

Minaj's performance at the 2010 Video Music Awards was an important highlight in her early career.

CHAPTER 1

A Rising Star

||||||||||||||||||||||||||||||||||||||||||||||||||||||||||||||||||||||||||

Nicki Minaj was a nervous wreck. It was September 12, 2010, three hours before her first live performance at the Video Music Awards (VMAs) on Music Television (MTV). She would be performing along with megastars such as Eminem and Justin Bieber, and the world would be watching.

Three days before, Minaj had smiled and joked around with her prep team in a Los Angeles, California, hotel room as they readied her look for the event. The stylist applied and reapplied makeup, a hairstylist adjusted her wig, and a tailor made alterations to the skintight purple bodysuit she would wear on stage.

As the event neared, however, Minaj's bubbly persona faded. She began to worry about failing. More than anything else, she worried she would let her family down. She knew the media could be ruthless. Just a few months earlier at the Black Entertainment Television (BET) Music Awards, Minaj had been accused of lip-synching. It was a performance she had trained hard for and had thought was a success. Minaj said the stinging accusations were untrue.

As Minaj stood in her dressing room preparing to take the stage, her mouth was set in a straight line. Her eyes were wide. The pink beehive-style

2010 BET AWARDS

Minaj won the Best Female Hip-Hop Artist award at the 2010 BET Awards, but it was overshadowed by rumors that she lip-synched her performance. To quell rumors, Minaj spoke out on the social networking site Twitter, tweeting that technical difficulties had caused problems with the sound.

Minaj performed at the 2010 BET Awards and was later accused of lip-synching.

wig made her look like a doll wearing a puff of cotton candy.

TAKING THE STAGE

But when she took to the stage, the scared little doll disappeared, and Minaj was nothing but calm, cool, and collected. As a pink metal ramp slowly lowered to reveal Minaj flanked by two backup dancers in similar purple leotards, the crowd whooped with excitement. In thigh-high, superhero-style boots, Minaj began to strut forward with confidence, stopping to dance every few steps. Hands on hips, she jutted her curvy hips out left, then right. She flashed a bright smile in one direction, then turned to growl in the other.

By the time rapper will.i.am joined her on stage to the tune of "Check It Out," she had already captured the crowd. Now the two of them were equals, playing off each other's verses and dance moves. Dressed head to toe in a black rubber pantsuit, will.i.am was on top of his game. But it was difficult to look away from the shimmering pink and purple pixie doing the monster walk next to him.

WILL.I.AM AND "CHECK IT OUT"

Though will.i.am has been rapping since the late 1980s and is also a producer and actor, he is perhaps best known as a member of the groundbreaking group the Black Eyed Peas. His collaboration with Minaj, "Check It Out," was featured on Minaj's first studio album, *Pink Friday,* and later remixed for his 2012 release, *#willpower.*

The VMA audience was fixated on Minaj as she began rapping in her signature low and speedy style. It was hard to recognize the girl who had quietly revealed her nervousness about the performance to an interviewer just hours before. Instead, she was powerful and animalistic. But when she heard the audience's roar of applause, her face broke out into an excited grin and she looked like herself again.

On stage, she clearly owned this party. Nicki Minaj was in charge.

THE FUTURE IS SO BRIGHT

Anyone watching the VMA performance could see how Minaj came alive onstage. She also impressed with her quick wit and sharp tongue as a featured rapper on singles with artists such as Kanye West and Drake. It was as if every song Minaj touched turned to gold. She set records with seven songs she collaborated on in the *Billboard* Hot 100 at once. Hip-hop, dance, and pop fans took notice as well, garnering her 1 million Twitter followers by August 2, 2010. Buzz swirled among hip-hop

HARAJUKU BARBIE

Much of Minaj's style is influenced by the Mattel Inc. fashion doll Barbie. Barbie is often associated with stereotypes about feminine beauty and is both publicly adored and criticized as a negative role model for young girls. Minaj's style tends to celebrate and parody the doll at the same time, reflecting both sides of the public debate around Barbie. Minaj also mixes her Barbie doll look with other inspirations, such as Harajuku, a style that gets its name from the fashion-forward district in Tokyo, Japan. Common characteristics of Harajuku style are bright colors, loud accessories, and an emphasis on things wacky or absurd. It is a playful style that does not take itself too seriously.

artists and music producers that Minaj was destined for stardom.

But despite Minaj's immediate success, some critics were skeptical. Minaj had not yet released her own full-length album. While her mixtapes were popular on the street, some felt her sound would not appeal to mainstream audiences. Critics speculated she might not be able to hold her own without the main attraction of superstar rappers such as Lil Wayne. Others criticized her outlandish appearance, commenting that her infamous stage costumes were ploys for media attention. Minaj said she wanted to empower women, but some criticized her lyrics and early mixtape covers as being too sexual.

Perhaps what was most fascinating about Minaj was that she burst onto the scene seemingly out of nowhere, but with a bang too loud for anyone to ignore. One music writer said, "She's kind of come to her fame in a curious way by being on other people's songs and by being sort of ubiquitous but only in a flash."[1] She became the most widely acclaimed and criticized female rapper in at least ten or 15 years.

Fans and critics alike waited anxiously for the release of Minaj's first studio album, *Pink Friday*, on November 19, 2010, just a few months after her VMA performance. Minaj's star threatened to burn

MIXTAPES

Beginning during the 1980s and 1990s, live hip-hop performances at parties or on the streets were often captured and distributed via rough recordings on audio tape, known as mixtapes. Today mixtapes are distributed on CDs or digital audio files and continue to be frequently traded and collected in the hip-hop community. They often feature rare or exclusive previously unreleased tracks or promote lesser-known artists.

out as quickly as it had risen if the record flopped. But a hit record could make the girl wearing wigs and calling herself "Barbie" unstoppable.

‖‖‖‖‖‖‖‖

Minaj's over-the-top style has attracted a lot of attention.

Nicki spent the first five years of her life in Trinidad.

CHAPTER 2

Little Girl in the Big Apple

nika Tanya Maraj was born on December 8, 1982, in Saint James, Port of Spain, on the Caribbean island of Trinidad. Like many Trinidadians, she came from a multicultural family, with mixed African and Indo-Asian ancestry. Her family included parents Carol and Robert and an older brother.

17

While Nicki, as friends and family called her, did not think of her family as poor growing up, they certainly lived in a crowded house. There were at least ten or 15 adults at all times living in her grandmother's three-bedroom home, as well as several pets.

When Nicki was three, her parents moved to New York City to find work and better opportunities for their family. They left young Nicki and her brother with their grandmother and other relatives in Trinidad. For the next two years, Nicki interacted with her parents mostly by telephone, and she only saw her mother during rare visits.

TRINIDAD AND TOBAGO

Trinidad and Tobago is a country made up of two Caribbean islands that lie off the northeastern coast of Venezuela. The capital of Trinidad and Tobago is Port of Spain, and the population is 1.3 million. The islands are rich in natural resources. Major exports include oil, coffee, sugar, and fruit, which support the economy along with tourism. The people primarily speak a Trinidadian Creole or Tobagonian Creole version of English. It is a multiethnic culture mainly of African and Indo-Asian descent.

Port of Spain is the capital of Trinidad and Tobago.

Though Nicki's grandmother was a loving mother figure to her, Nicki missed her parents—and her mother in particular—all the time. Nicki remembers wanting to be with her mother so much that when Carol would visit, Nicki would get dressed and pack in the middle of the night so she was ready to go along when her mother left.

During one of Carol's visits, four-year-old Nicki was hospitalized with a hernia. When it was time for Carol to return to the United States after five days, Nicki just looked down and could not smile when her mother kissed her good-bye. Crestfallen, Nicki sang a song to her mother with the lyrics

"Every time you go away, you take a piece of me with you."[1] Hearing these sad lyrics coming out of tiny Nicki was so heartbreaking that her mother cried through the entire six-hour flight back to New York.

By 1988, when Nicki was five, her parents were both employed and housed in New York. At last, Nicki and her brother could be with their parents.

Dressed in a pink corduroy jacket with a fur hood and wooden buttons, Nicki looked out the window of the airplane as they were about to land in New York City. "Look!" said her mother, "Snow!"[2] Having grown up in hot, humid Trinidad, Nicki had never seen snow before. She was thrilled.

TROUBLE IN PARADISE

But the holiday only lasted a brief period. Far from the white picket fences Nicki had seen in television and movies, her family lived in South Jamaica, Queens. It was a crime-ridden and dangerous borough of the city, and the family lived there during the height of the crack cocaine epidemic. Robert had not wanted to leave Trinidad in the first

In 1983, crack cocaine first became available on the street in New York City. Crack was a highly potent and inexpensive smokable form of powdered cocaine. According to the US Drug Enforcement Agency (DEA), in major cities such as New York City, one dosage unit of crack cost $2.50. Because it was so inexpensive, high rates of crack usage grew in poor neighborhoods. The crack epidemic was particularly brutal for populations from the Dominican Republic and other Caribbean nations residing in New York City. Crack addiction was often wholly debilitating, leading to murders, theft, child abandonment, and damage to unborn fetuses, who became known as "crack babies."

place, and the transition to life in the United States was difficult for him. Shortly after the kids arrived, he lost his job and began drinking and using drugs.

As his drug use grew worse, his behavior became more erratic and volatile. Soon fighting filled the household as Robert frequently turned his anger toward Carol. During one scary incident, a drugged Robert even attempted to set the house on fire with Carol in it. From then on, Nicki and her brother lived in constant fear that their father would kill their mother.

Carol continued working long hours as a nurse's aid to earn money for the family and hold everything together. But she could tell the fighting and abuse were having a negative impact on her daughter. "It was a devastating period in our lives," she has said.[3] When her father was violent against her mother, little Nicki often tried to stand between them with her hands on her hips to prevent him from hurting her. Today, the grown Nicki often displays this tough girl stance while performing.

MAKING ART FROM PAIN

To escape the turmoil, Nicki began fantasizing about living a different life. She dreamed of becoming rich so she could save her family from its horrible situation. She started developing different personas and speaking in different voices, which enlivened her fantasyland, a place where Nicki says she still "finds pleasure."[4]

By the time Nicki entered Elizabeth Blackwell Middle School 210 in the Ozone Park area of Queens, she was ready to begin putting her imagination to greater use. Though the school was well known in New York for "being big and being bad,"[5] Nicki was lucky enough to meet her favorite teacher, Elizabeth Smith, there. Smith encouraged Nicki and her fifth-grade classmates to create and act out elaborate plays with costumes and sets.

Plays such as *Keeping the Peace* required the students to use examples from their own experience—such as a fight at school over a broken pencil—to think about bigger issues like peace and understanding between neighbors. Nicki shined in the play, earning high praise from her school principal and her parents. The experience was hugely rewarding for her and a welcome escape from her tumultuous home life.

Around the same time, 12-year-old Nicki wrote her first rap. Inspired by an older girl in her neighborhood who also rapped, Nicki wrote, "Cookie's the name, chocolate chip is the flavor /

WILD HAIRSTYLES

Now famous for her wild and artistic wigs, Nicki first became obsessed with hairstyling when she was just nine years old. Brushing and gelling her hair into extreme styles became another form of self-expression for her. Once, when asked why she had "messed up" her hair, she replied, "I'm someone new with this hair."[6]

Suck up my style like a cherry Life Saver."[7] The older girl made her repeat it over and over again to all the kids in the neighborhood. Though she later suspected they had been making fun of her, rapping in public helped her get used to performing. Soon Nicki was sure she knew what she wanted to do with her life—she would become an actor and perform all the time.

||||||||||

Nicki used acting and rapping as escapes from her difficult childhood.

Nicki's high school inspired the 1980 film *Fame*.

CHAPTER 3

I'm an Actor!

||||||||||||||||||||||||||||||||||||||||||||||||||||||||||||||||||

To kick-start her acting career, Nicki applied to Fiorello H. LaGuardia High School of Music & Art and Performing Arts, which inspired the Broadway musical and 1980 film *Fame*. A remake of *Fame* was released in 2009. LaGuardia was a competitive school to get into, and Nicki would have to audition for both singing and acting as part of her application.

On the day of her audition in 1996, Nicki found she had lost her voice.

LaGuardia Arts is famous for churning out famous actors, dancers, and artists. Famous alumni include actor/producer Wesley Snipes, rapper Slick Rick, designer Isaac Mizrahi, and Oscar-winning actors Robert DeNiro and Adrien Brody. Nicki claims that LaGuardia lived up to its artsy reputation, with kids jumping up on tables to sing, dancing in the hallways, and wearing outlandish outfits.

She sang for the judges anyway, and was devastated when it did not go well. She quickly decided to give up on LaGuardia altogether, thinking, "Forget this stupid school, I don't want to be here anyway . . ."[1] She begged her mother to take her home, but to her surprise, her mother put her foot down, forcing her to stay and go through with her drama audition.

At her mother's urging, Nicki gathered the courage to go on stage, where her worries quickly disappeared. She felt at home, and it seemed the judges thought it was the right place for her too. Of the experience, Nicki has said, "That's what defines a true leader or boss. It's being able to bounce back."[2] Nicki was accepted to study drama at LaGuardia.

TEEN DREAM

Over the next four years, Nicki flourished. Outspoken and confident, she was a natural leader. Though some students found her intimidating, she made them laugh by singing in funny voices, speaking in a British accent, and adding a *B* to the front of everyone's name. "Andrew" became "Bandrew" and "Ashley" became "Bashley."

"You could tell at LaGuardia what someone's major was based on their behavior, and Nicki was definitely a drama major."[3]

—*NICKI MINAJ'S FORMER CLASSMATE*

Always a wild card, Nicki could be a bit of a troublemaker. She got into a few fights with other girls at school and took her dad's car out before she had a license to drive. On one such occasion when she was 16, Nicki got into a fender bender. The police showed up at her house to inform her parents of what she had done. Her parents were not pleased, but Nicki took responsibility for fixing the car, spending all her savings from her summer job.

LaGuardia was also where Nicki first became interested in fashion. Although her typical style included the popular baggy Tommy Hilfiger shirts and Boss jeans of the time, she was always attracted to a dramatic, dressed-up look. When she was a teenager, she met a glamorous woman who wore heels, makeup, and pantsuits. From then on, she began to incorporate these styles into her wardrobe.

By her senior year, Nicki had attracted the eye of her teachers and talent scouts. Talent scouts typically sought out the best and brightest of LaGuardia's graduates and helped them launch their careers. At the final showcase for Nicki's senior class, she received approximately ten business cards from Manhattan scouts who were interested in representing her as she tried her hand as a working actor.

EARLY INSPIRATIONS

Some of Nicki Minaj's early musical influences included musical sensation Diana Ross and 1980s pop singer Cyndi Lauper. As a high school student, she loved singer Lauryn Hill, even quoting one of her songs under her photo in her high school yearbook: "To survive is to stay alive in the face of opposition."[4]

WORKING GIRL

Nicki graduated from LaGuardia in 2000. She was ready to hit the ground running, but acting jobs were harder to come by than she had hoped. She began working as a waitress at Red Lobster to pay for a car and apartment rent. But it was clear waitressing was not exactly Nicki's dream job. Her childhood friend Thembi Banks said, "Some people are just not meant to serve."[5]

While waitressing in 2001, Nicki tried to break into acting by auditioning for off-off-Broadway productions—smaller productions in theaters with fewer than 100 seats. Nicki got an opportunity to act in one of these productions, a play called *In Case You Forget*. Like her cast mates, Nicki was "young, hungry, with stuff to prove."[6] She would rehearse each evening after her shift at Red Lobster still wearing her uniform.

Though the play was a great experience, Nicki struggled to find work and began to lose her passion for acting. Freestyling had been a favorite hobby throughout high school, and Nicki set her sights on rapping professionally.

Nicki developed an early interest in fashion and acting, which she has incorporated into her musical performances.

She continued to work nine to five at various jobs, but now she was devoting her off hours to promoting herself as a rapper, distributing demo tapes and trying to get a record deal. She worked hard to meet the right people in the business, too.

NOT GONNA DO IT ANYMORE

Finally, after getting fired from another day job she didn't care about, Nicki told her mom she planned to devote all her time to becoming a rap artist. Her mom was worried she wouldn't make it, but Nicki persisted: "I don't care if I end up in a shelter, I'm not going back to work."[7]

From then on she focused all her attention on her craft. Her parents would find her sitting in the car, listening to her demo tapes over and over again and writing lyrics. She also developed a relationship with a production company that gave her free studio time, and she recorded as much as she could.

In 2002, Nicki met industry-insider LouStar, head of the New York City-based rap group Hoodstars. LouStar was the son of Bow-Legged Lou, also known as Lou George, a member of the legendary rap group Full Force. LouStar took a special interest in Nicki; he thought she was special. He helped her record the song "Autobiography," in which she rapped about her traumatic childhood. Of the experience, Nicki said writing and recording became her "only escape."[8] With Lou and others behind her, Nicki plowed ahead in her pursuit of fame. One way or another, she was determined to make a name for herself.

IIIIIIIII

Nicki had to work hard to break into the music industry.

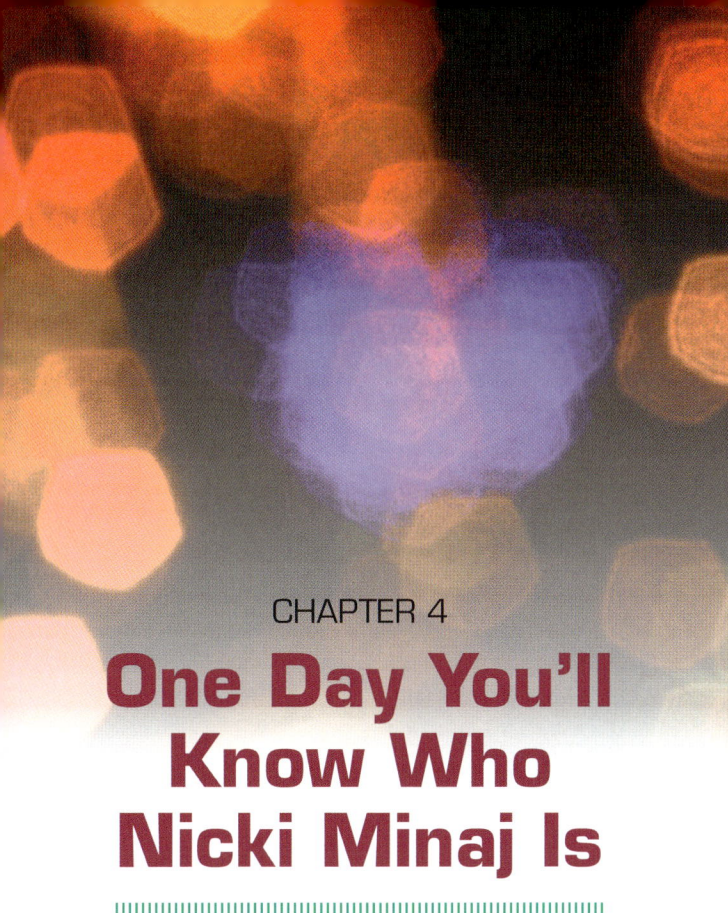

CHAPTER 4

One Day You'll Know Who Nicki Minaj Is

||||||||||||||||||||||||||||||||||||||||||||||||||||||||||||||||||||||||||

The next few years were full of hard work and hustling for Nicki. Aside from her relationship with LouStar, she promoted most of her own music. Finally, she decided to branch out from the Hoodstars.

In 2006, Nicki started a MySpace social-networking page, posting recordings of her raps and songs. Fans of her page started downloading her tracks. Eventually, she was able to perform her own show and fill a club to capacity at 200 audience members, solely consisting of fans from MySpace.

NEW NAME, NEW FAN BASE

The buzz from Nicki's MySpace page attracted the attention of Fendi, the chief executive officer (CEO) of Dirty Money Records. Fendi was well respected by the hip-hop community, known for using his connections to help unknown artists gain recognition and sometimes get a record deal.

Fendi loved her look and sound immediately, but he also wanted to make some changes to her image. At the time Nicki was using her real last name, Maraj. Fendi encouraged her to change it to Minaj instead. He began featuring her in *The Come Up,* a DVD series of rising stars in hip-hop.

The Come Up DVDs were sold primarily on the streets and showcased exclusive videos and freestyle footage. Fendi and *The Come Up* provided Minaj a platform to promote her music to a wider audience.

DVDs featuring Minaj soon spread rapidly among hip-hop fans. In one video, Minaj addresses her fans: "What up, everybody? It's Nicki Minaj. I just want to say thank you for the support. At the end of the day, I am the baddest b***h in the game."[1] Her confidence was infectious. With new footage coming out every few months, Minaj gained a significant following.

||||||||||||||||||||||||||||||||||||||||||||||||||||||||

"WARNING" ||||||||||||||||||||||||||||||||||||||||||||||||||||||||||||||||||||||||||||||||||||||||||||||||

One song Minaj performed on *The Come Up* DVD was "Warning." It was a cover of a song from the Notorious B.I.G.'s 1994 debut album *Ready to Die*. "Warning" was the promotional track for *Ready to Die*, which achieved massive success and platinum sales. It turned the Notorious B.I.G. into an overnight success. *Time* included the album on its list of the 100 greatest albums of all time in 2006. In 1997, Notorious B.I.G. died prematurely at age 25 after an unknown assailant killed him in a drive-by shooting. He died just two weeks before the release of his album *Life After Death*.

Rapper Lil Wayne took Minaj under his wing.

LIL WAYNE IS CALLING

The Come Up series resulted in Minaj's big break. In 2007, the cover of one of the DVDs featured hip-hop superstar Lil Wayne. Lil Wayne had never heard of Minaj, but on the DVD, her video appeared directly after his. Some in the industry speculated Fendi purposely placed the video to help promote Minaj.

Lil Wayne noticed Minaj immediately. He recalls, "I was like, 'This female right here is amazing . . . Get me in contact with that girl named Nicki.'"[2] Minaj was also eager to meet Lil Wayne, whom she described as being "smitten" with her.[3] Soon after, she flew to Los Angeles and met him in his studio.

During the meeting, the two discussed Lil Wayne's label Young Money, which operated as a collective and included up-and-coming hip-hop artists similar to Minaj. Even though the label had no female artists, Lil Wayne had a hunch Minaj would be a good addition to the Young Money crew.

LIL WAYNE

Born Dwayne Michael Carter Jr. on September 27, 1982, in New Orleans, Louisiana, Lil Wayne began rapping at the age of nine with Cash Money Records. During the mid-1990s, Lil Wayne made a name for himself in hip-hop by releasing a variety of mixtapes and singles and rapping on other artists' songs. He has collaborated with many artists, including T. I., Chris Brown, Akon, Eminem, Birdman, Rick Ross, Jay-Z, and Kanye West, and has won four Grammy Awards. Minaj refers to Lil Wayne as her "sensei," a Japanese word that means teacher, master, or mentor.[4]

Hip-hop and rap collectives such as Young Money are groups of musicians in which membership is flexible and the artists share creative control. Collectives act as support systems, allowing individual artists to grow in a comfortable and collaborative environment. Members of collectives also collaborate on one another's tracks and albums. Some hip-hop collectives eventually become record labels, allowing them to promote their artists. One collective-turned-record-label is Bad Boy Records, which was founded in 1993 by popular rapper/producer Sean "Diddy" Combs. Another is Ruff Ryders, founded in 1988, which managed up-and-coming rappers such as DMX, Ma$e, The Lox, and female rapper Eve. The Ruff Ryders label disbanded in 2010.

ATLANTA, HERE COMES NICKI

Shortly after her initial meeting with Lil Wayne in 2007, Minaj relocated to Atlanta, Georgia, where she quickly became involved in the local music scene. In Atlanta, Minaj felt she "had a family [that] welcomed me with open arms."[5] Minaj hired Atlanta-based Debra Antney as her manager. She soon became a big name around town, filling clubs night after night. Some weeks she performed up to four shows.

The move away from New York was not only a boost for Minaj's rap career, it was also liberating for her personally. She loved her family and was particularly close to her mother, but New York was also filled with bad memories. She relished the opportunity to make a name for herself in a new town.

Minaj was at the top of her game, but it was only the beginning. Soon she would split much of her time between Atlanta and Los Angeles while working more closely with Lil Wayne and the Young Money crew. Wayne saw her talent and thought Minaj had the spark it took to be a star.

|||||||||||

ATLANTA HIP-HOP SCENE

Atlanta, Georgia, has become a mecca for young, successful, and wealthy African Americans. Perhaps this was one reason Minaj felt support for her ambitions while she lived there. Atlanta is home to singer-songwriter Cee Lo Green, hip-hop megastar and Minaj collaborator Gucci Mane, and rapper 2 Chainz, who collaborated with Minaj on her 2012 song "Beez in the Trap." In recent years, according to a writer for the *New York Times,* Atlanta rap has "moved from the margins to becoming hip-hop's center of gravity,"[6] with abundant fans and multiple producers seeking out new talent.

Rapper Missy Elliott was an
early inspiration to Minaj.

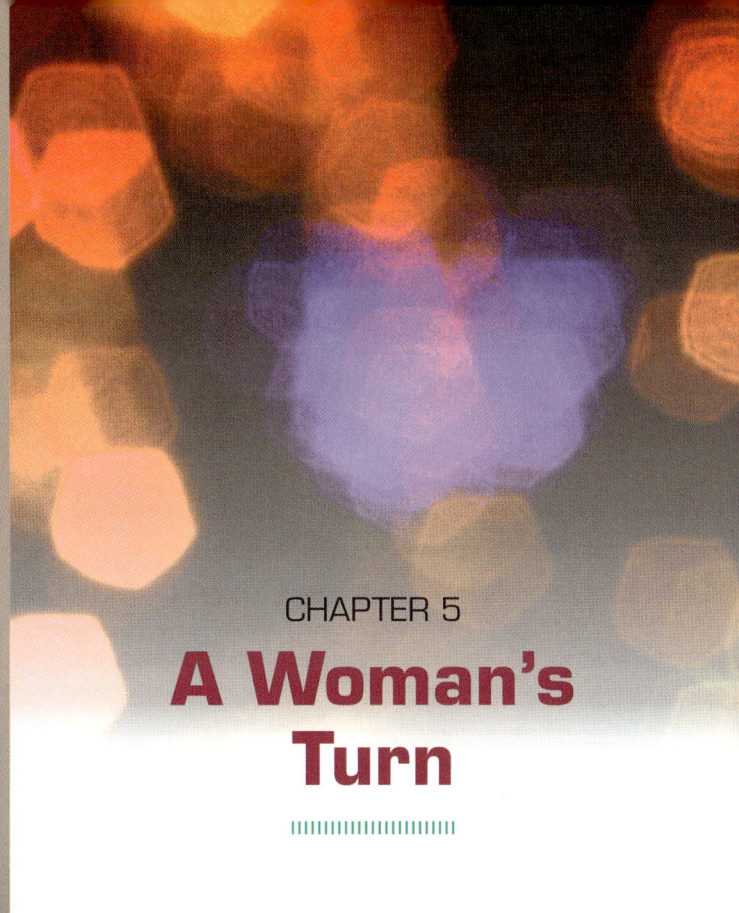

CHAPTER 5

A Woman's Turn

||||||||||||||||||||||||||

For Minaj, being a woman in the hip-hop world was both a blessing and a curse. When she first appeared on the scene, few women were performing and seriously promoting themselves as rap artists. Compared to the number of male rappers performing and selling millions of albums, there weren't very many famous female rappers. Among them were Lil' Kim, Missy Elliott, and Lauryn Hill, who were

Minaj has said Lil Wayne, *left*, was the first person in hip-hop to support her creative spirit.

some of Minaj's idols. On one hand, it was difficult to get people to take her seriously. But Minaj was also able to stand out as unique and special because there were so few women in the game.

Minaj was keenly aware that as a female rapper she received different treatment than her male counterparts. For one thing, she knew she would be judged more for her looks and body, and she had two obvious options for how to handle this inequality. She could exploit her sexuality to gain attention but risk not being taken seriously for her talent in the long term. Or, she could reject the sexed-up image of herself and demand to be taken seriously as more than just a pretty face.

But Minaj was not comfortable with either choice. Over the next few years, she publicly battled the dilemma of being a female rapper. There were times when Minaj seemed to embrace the sexual iconography completely by adopting the Barbie persona or dressing skimpily. At other times, however, she would appear to be strong

SUPPORTING WOMEN

Besides having a feud with Lil' Kim, Minaj refuses to put down other women in order to get ahead. She wrote the song "Still I Rise" to get women to see how they can help themselves by helping one another:

"Every time a door opens for me / That means you just got a better opportunity to do you / Better understand these labels look at numbers and statistics / I win, you win, it's just logistics."[1]

and fearless, even using male characters to express herself in her music.

While Minaj experimented with complex gender issues in her music and style, one thing became clearer. Minaj had the connections to achieve her goal of becoming a rap music front woman. She was in a unique position to take advantage of the fact that virtually no other female rappers like her existed on the scene. If it was time for a woman to take over hip-hop, Minaj seemed like the artist to do it.

||||||||||||||||||||||||||||||||||||||||||||||||||||||||

THE MIXTAPES

Lil Wayne sensed that bringing a strong female into his crew could lead to big possibilities. Once Minaj began working with him, her career took off quickly. Over the next few years, Wayne helped Minaj record and release three mixtapes.

The first of Minaj's mixtapes, *Playtime Is Over*, was released in July 2007. During the photo shoot for the mixtape promo, Minaj began playing with her new Barbie persona. Wearing a pink and yellow striped bikini, large hoop earrings, and long curled hair, she declared, "I'm a star! Having said that, I'm also a Barbie doll, and Barbie dolls are cute."[2] The Barbie style was an unexpected contrast to the often raw, sexy, and hard sounds of her music.

For the cover image of her second mixtape, *Sucka Free*, released in April 2008, Minaj amped up the sex appeal. Minaj wore an open hoodie with nothing but a bra and underwear underneath and licked a lollipop suggestively. The photo of Minaj was meant to be reminiscent of the promotional photo rapper Lil' Kim used for her 1996 album *Hard Core*.

LIL' KIM

Lil' Kim, one of the most successful female rappers of all time, was one of Minaj's early influences. During the summer of 2010, Minaj finally reached her idol's mark when her song "Your Love" became the first by a female rapper to reach Number 1 on the *Billboard* rap chart since Lil' Kim's cameo on 50 Cent's "Magic Stick" in 2003. Lil' Kim has since called Minaj a "clone."[3] Minaj retorted that Lil' Kim is a "sore loser."[4] Minaj also pointed out that while Lil' Kim once paved the way for her in hip-hop music, Minaj is now doing the same for Lil' Kim. Regarding the clash, Lil Wayne notes that jealousy and resentment are part of the game of hip-hop fame: "That crown is heavy and right now she has that on her head."[5]

Minaj later said she regretted taking her image to such extremes of overt sexuality, saying, "It was too soon for that. Not even too soon—it was unnecessary."[6] She worried she might be sending the wrong message to her young female fan base. Plus, her worry that the music industry might dismiss her as just another attractive girl—instead of a true artist—continued to nag at her.

Despite the regrettable cover, Minaj continued expanding her impressive resume. Around the same time as *Playtime Is Over* and *Sucka Free* came out, she appeared on Lil Wayne's 2007 mixtape, *Da Drought 3*. Wayne and Minaj's tapes were distributed widely among fans and newcomers to her music, earning critical acclaim.

While attracting the attention of an ever-growing fan base, Minaj decided to step up to the plate as a serious artist. For her next mixtape, *Beam Me Up, Scotty*, Minaj decided to downplay the explicit photos that were so noticeable on *Sucka Free*. The cover of *Beam Me Up, Scotty* featured Minaj dressed like the superhero Wonder Woman. Even though she was still showing a lot of skin, her image evoked humor, fantasy, and drama rather than solely sex appeal.

Though Minaj no longer deliberately over-sexualizes herself in photos and videos, she continues to receive plenty of attention for her body. Not all of it is good. In recent years, rumors circulated that Minaj received surgical implants to achieve her proportionally larger backside. Minaj refuses to discuss the rumors—or her backside— in interviews.

In *Beam Me Up, Scotty*, released in April 2009, Minaj also departed from the sexual lyrics that were so obvious on her first two mixtapes. She recorded diverse vocal stylings, introducing listeners to new characters. Lil Wayne described the sound as "pure, uncut, raw . . . she was going a mile a minute."[7] In addition to Lil Wayne, her mixtape featured other standout performers such as Gucci Mane and Busta Rhymes.

When *Beam Me Up, Scotty* reached critics' ears, they went wild. Minaj was delivering something fresh and exciting, something no other woman in hip-hop was doing. One critic said, "She was real rough with it . . . she had that edge . . . [and] swagger and her confidence was through the roof."[8]

LEARNING CURVE

Shortly after the release of *Beam Me Up, Scotty* in August 2009, Minaj was officially signed to Young Money Entertainment. Not only was Minaj the first female to join the crew, her deal with Young Money—an affiliate of leading multinational company Universal Music—was exceptionally favorable to her as an artist. In it, she retained her 360 rights. This meant Minaj owned any product promotions, appearances, or other income derived from merchandise, tours, or publishing.

Lil Wayne had appeared on each of her mixtapes. Now Minaj's working partnership with him was official, and his role as her mentor had deepened. In addition to coaching her

WHY 360 RIGHTS MATTER

Appearances and endorsements are a part of the business of being Nicki Minaj. Today, it is common for artists with brands as big as Minaj's to give up their 360 rights in exchange for promotion by the record labels that put out their music. By retaining her rights, Minaj controls what products she endorses, where and when she makes appearances, and any income that results from the Minaj brand. She can reportedly pocket more than $30,000 for rapping at a nightclub.

on rap stylings and vocals, he also taught her some important lessons on making it in the music business.

On one occasion, Minaj learned a lesson she would not forget about how to treat studio time on Wayne's clock. The crew was hard at work recording the song "Bedrock," which was to be the second single on their debut album as the collective Young Money Entertainment. She wanted to be featured on the song, but she made an amateur mistake. She left during the middle of recording her cameo to fly out of town for a show. When she returned to the studio, she was surprised to find Wayne was angry with her. He quickly made it clear that her departure was unprofessional. In her absence, Wayne had removed her cameo from "Bedrock."

Minaj was crushed, but she was determined to change Wayne's mind. She wrote lyrics for her verse anyway and begged him to listen to them. Luckily, Wayne liked her enough to forgive her mistake, and Minaj was allowed back on the song. When it was released on March 22, 2010, "Bedrock" reached Number 2 on the *Billboard* Hot 100 and was the collective's biggest hit to date.

But Minaj had little time to relax and celebrate the success. The hype generated from her mixtapes and her feature in the "Bedrock" single meant she would soon be the most in-demand female hip-hop artist in the industry. Wayne said to her, "Everyone is gonna want you on their song. . . . This is a big deal. . . . Do you understand what this is gonna mean?"[9] The new "It" girl of hip-hop braced herself for the long and exciting journey ahead.

||||||||||

Lil Wayne and Minaj perform together on New Year's Eve 2011.

Minaj performs with rapper Ludacris on BET in February 2010.

CHAPTER 6

The "It" Girl of Hip-Hop

With a fantastic record deal and a single under her belt, Minaj was well on her way to fame and fortune. She was also beginning to reveal her savvy business side to those in the music industry. While Minaj was playful on stage, she was serious in the studio. Unlike many other artists, she preferred to wake up early and work during regular business hours. Her workday usually began at 9 or 10 a.m. While she was working, Minaj kept to herself. She could often be found holed up in a corner, furiously writing verses. She was not known for chatting or goofing around.

> "Wayne is the least shy person in the entire world. He loves to be the center of attention. He eats it for dinner. And that's why I was so drawn to him."[1]
>
> —NICKI MINAJ ON LIL WAYNE

Minaj had the most coveted voice in female rap and a reputation for professionalism, and Lil Wayne's prediction proved true. Virtually everyone wanted to work with Minaj. As the calls came in, she appeared with singer Robin Thicke on *The David Letterman Show* in February 2010 for a performance of Thicke's song "Shakin' It 4 Daddy." She was also featured on the song "Lil Freak" by singer Usher in March 2010.

In the video for rapper Ludacris's "My Chick Bad," which premiered on BET on

February 19, 2010, Minaj showed her zany side. Minaj wore claws similar to Freddy Krueger's, an iconic horror movie character. Her dance moves were jerky and her voice otherworldly. Her theatrical and costumed approach to the video surprised viewers in a good way. Everyone wanted to see what she would do next. For Minaj, shooting the video was a liberating return to her roots as an actor. Of the experience, she said, "It made me feel so free. It was me inside."[2] A personal as well as commercial success, "My Chick Bad" climbed the *Billboard* Hot 100 to Number 11.

In February 2010, Minaj was flattered when singer Mariah Carey asked her to collaborate on the song "Up Out My Face." The song and video could be characterized as very girly. Minaj and Carey play best friends, bonding over failed

MARIAH CAREY |||||||||||||||||||||||||||||||||||||||||||||||||||||||||||||||||||||||||||||

According to the Recording Industry Association of America (RIAA), singer Mariah Carey is the third best-selling female artist of all time, after singers Madonna and Barbara Streisand. Since debuting in 1990, Carey has won five Grammys as of June 2012, and has expanded her career to include acting, producing, fashion, and cosmetics. Like Minaj, Carey grew up in a multiethnic family in New York City.

relationships with men, dressed in cocktail dresses and nurse's uniforms with puppies and balloons as props. It was not a commercial success, but the collaboration was further evidence that Minaj's options in the music world were expanding. She had a place with rappers and pop stars alike.

Minaj's feature on Christina Aguilera's song "Woohoo" in May 2010 was yet another opportunity to align herself with a leading female in music and stretch her talents beyond the hip-hop realm. The song reached the Top 100 in US charts.

Minaj's work with a variety of artists expanded her appeal. Often, the songs that featured her grew popular very quickly and enjoyed mainstream success. *Vibe* wrote she was "as popular with rap's tough guys as . . . teenage girls."[3]

MASSIVE ATTACK, COLOSSAL FAILURE

Almost everything Minaj touched turned to gold—but not everything. Throughout her big successes in 2009 and 2010, Cash Money Records

Rapper Sean Garrett appeared in the expensive music video for "Massive Attack."

and Motown Records threw weight and money behind an unusual video for her single "Massive Attack," featuring rapper Sean Garrett. The video also featured recording artist/actor Drake and rap scenester Amber Rose, a former girlfriend of rapper Kanye West.

Filmed in March 2010, the video contained an over-the-top desert adventure complete with giant tanks, explosions, and car crashes. Minaj appeared as characters ranging from a Harajuku-style soldier to a wild jungle cat to a ninja. Both the song and the video failed to tell a consistent story.

The producers and label executives had no idea what to make of it.

The industry considered the entire project an expensive flop. In addition to costs, damage to a rented Lamborghini while shooting the video's final escape scene resulted in a lawsuit. The repairs totaled approximately $12,000. Some critics wondered if Minaj was destined to be "Queen Cameo" rather than a solo artist.

> "My goal the whole time has been for people to see me as a stand-alone artist. I came out with Young Money, the biggest hip-hop label in the world at that time. And then it was, 'How do I branch away from Lil Wayne?'"[4]
>
> —NICKI MINAJ

Not only was the video a bust, costing $50,000, but the song was also dropped from Minaj's upcoming album, *Pink Friday*. Still, there were a few positives to the experience. It showed that Young Money supported Minaj's creativity even at times when it was not marketable. Minaj also proved she had the strength to stand up for her own vision even when it did not match what others, namely industry powerhouses, wanted.

Her unwillingness to back down in the face of adversity would serve her well in the coming months. As Minaj's fame grew, so did criticism in the industry and media. She would need a tough skin to withstand the ever-building pressure.

SHE'S GOT THE BEST VERSE

Minaj regained her footing after the "Massive Attack" setback when she appeared on Kanye West's song "Monster" in September 2010. The song also featured indie rocker Bon Iver and hip-hop megastars Jay-Z, Charlie Wilson, and Rick Ross. It became a critical and commercial success, reaching Number 18 on the *Billboard* Hot 100.

Beyond ratings, "Monster" was also an important professional milestone for Minaj. Working with some of the top performers in the industry was a huge honor. Minaj did not disappoint, impressing her collaborators in the studio with her ability to write and rap on the spot. Her verse was also recognized as the best one on the track. Ross even went as far as to describe Minaj as "one of the greatest" rappers of all time.[5]

> "Ok, first things first, I'll eat your brains / Then I'mma start rocking gold teeth and fangs."[6]
>
> —FROM MINAJ'S "MONSTER" VERSE

Around the same time, Minaj flexed her professional muscles yet again. She cut ties with Antney as her manager and immediately began working with Sean "Diddy" Combs and James Cruz from Violator Management. Minaj ended up parting ways with Combs and Cruz in May 2011, beginning a relationship with Lil Wayne's management team instead. She also settled in Los Angeles permanently, finding the weather and atmosphere better for writing music.

IT'S ALL RIDING ON THE SOLO RECORD

On October 8, 2010, Minaj had set a *Billboard* record. With seven Hot 100 hits, she became the

Minaj's star was rising in 2010.

first female solo artist to have that many singles on the *Billboard* chart at the same time. All signs pointed to Minaj becoming the next superstar in music. But there was one big question remaining.

Despite her success, Minaj had yet to prove she was an artist in her own right. She had not produced a full-length album, and her solo effort "Massive Attack" had failed. For the time being, succeeding with her solo record was Minaj's biggest task. Everything was riding on *Pink Friday*.

Minaj has developed a supportive
friendship with rapper Drake.

CHAPTER 7

Who Is Nicki Minaj?

IIIIIIIIIIIIIIIIIIIIIIIIIIIIIIIIIIIIIII

As news spread that Minaj had broken a *Billboard* record for the most songs in the Hot 100 at one time by a female solo artist, anticipation for *Pink Friday* continued to build. Critics and fans started to wonder about the real Minaj, who had gained fame so quickly that her success almost seemed premeditated by a record executive. Her tendency to use alter egos alongside her "real" voice also confused people. Some began calling her a fake.

At the same time, Minaj was grappling with her own success. She visited her old neighborhood in Queens, and the community was proud of her. She was happy to be a living example of success that others could aspire to. But Minaj also felt some guilt, wondering whether she deserved her success more than the other struggling artists she had grown up with.

> **"On the inside that's how I feel . . . the bubbly kid that wants to play."[1]**
>
> —NICKI MINAJ

Minaj found support in her growing friendship with fellow Young Money rapper Drake. Similar to Minaj, Drake was experiencing an enormous amount of success very quickly. The two bonded over their shared history as high school performers. Minaj said of their relationship: "Drake and I are embracing the fact that we went to school, we love acting, we love theater, and that's ok—and it's especially good for the black community to know that's ok, that's embraced."[2] Minaj also played a sisterly role, encouraging Drake to maintain his clean-cut look. The rising stars closed out 2010 with their smash hit collaboration "Moment 4 Life" in December.

||||||||||||||||||||||||||||||||||||||||||||||||||||||||||||

STRICTLY BUSINESS

While the buzz surrounding her record escalated, Minaj did her best to cope with the pressure. She logged long hours in the studio, which she kept heated to a steamy 90 degrees Fahrenheit (32° C). She sustained herself on healthful snacks such as cranberries, almonds, and water.

Minaj became increasingly interested in all aspects of the music business related to selling her record. She wanted to know how sales were conducted, how discs and merchandise were manufactured, and from where they would be shipped. Most artists leave the business side of their records to their managers and producers. But Minaj was intent on understanding all the details, such as the breakdown of base costs versus profits for her records and promotional stints.

The stakes got higher for Minaj as her fame exploded. She became highly protective of her public image, saying, "I am the marketer and promoter of the Nicki Minaj brand."[3] She chose her own video choreography and styled herself for photo shoots. Above all, Minaj was a perfectionist. She trusted herself more than anyone else to represent her vision.

The desire to control her brand and business deals stemmed from Minaj's determination to learn the business side of the music industry. Minaj developed a reputation for being tough when she made deals. She has turned down offers to do features for other artists when she was recording her own music. She has also walked out of photo shoots when the clothes and food services weren't up to her professional standards.

> "I hate cameras. I hate cameras and I hate camera phones. The camera's my worst enemy and my best friend. It's the way I convey emotions to the world without saying a word, so I use it. People always say, 'You come alive as soon as the camera's on.'"[4]
>
> —NICKI MINAJ

Minaj posed with two of her fans in November 2010.

Some in the industry have given Minaj flak for being difficult or demanding. But Minaj has responded, "You have to be like a beast—that's the only way they respect you."[5] She resented that she was called nasty names for standing up for herself while her male peers got more respect. But she hoped this no-nonsense attitude would set a precedent, causing her to be treated like the superstar she planned to become.

Despite her reputation for being tough, Minaj was anything but intimidating when it came to her fans. She chose to communicate regularly via social media, particularly Twitter. Minaj's Twitter account grew to more than 2 million followers in 2010. Minaj's exchanges with her fans on Twitter were often personal. When fans wrote to her that they were struggling with problems similar to those she did growing up, such as abuse and drug use in their families, Minaj provided encouragement and loving words. She consistently advised them to stay in school.

Minaj's direct connection with her fans certainly helped the success of her album. Six weeks before its release, *Pink Friday* sold enough copies to be the Number 4 rap and hip-hop record on Amazon.com.

||||||||||||||||||||||||||||||||||||||||||||||||||

FANS ||||||||||||||||||||||||||||||||||||||||||||||||||||||||||||||||||||||||||||||||||||||||||||

Minaj tries to keep a close relationship with her fans. Once she was at Negril Restaurant in New York City, "and I brought, like, ten of the fans who were waiting outside with me, and bought them all food!"[6]

PINK FRIDAY EXPLOSION

On November 23, 2010, the album everyone was waiting to hear was finally released. Within days, it became clear *Pink Friday* would be a wild success. The record sold more than 400,000 copies within the first week. The critical acclaim that accompanied the incredible sales silenced anyone who doubted Minaj's ability to put out a successful album. DJ Diamond Kuts described the album as a classic, because "She gives you the funny side . . . she gives you the serious side, and she gives you phenomenal music."[7]

One of the most entertaining aspects of *Pink Friday* is the variety of wild and new characters Minaj created to sing the different verses in her songs. Sometimes the characters communicate with each other to tell a story, similar to the dramatic plays Minaj acted in as a teenager. Her main character, Roman Zolanski, is described as Minaj's "gay male alter ego."[8] In the song "Roman's Revenge," Roman is angry and crazy, with Minaj singing his parts in a low, growling voice. She also introduces the character of his mother, Martha, to chastise him when he is a "bad boy," saying things like "Roman, stop it. You've gone mad, I say, mad."[9]

> "I'm not Jasmine, I'm Aladdin . . . I'm startin' to feel like a dungeon dragon / Raah Raah . . ."[10]
>
> —MINAJ AS ROMAN IN "ROMAN'S REVENGE"

Minaj's collaborators join in the theatrics on *Pink Friday*. Her character, Nicki Lewinsky, has a relationship with Lil Wayne's character, President Carter. Other characters on the album are "Nicki the Ninja" and "Harajuku Barbie." In addition to straight rap, Minaj also incorporates elements of pop and dance music.

These characters allowed Minaj to play with different sides of her own personality—feminine, boyish, aggressive, and demure—making the record eclectic and fun to listen to. The success of *Pink Friday* earned Minaj the award for Favorite Hip-Hop Artist and Favorite Hip-Hop Album at the 2011 American Music Awards on November 21, 2011. Minaj had finally created the masterpiece of her dreams.

Minaj hosted a party in November 2010 leading up to the debut of *Pink Friday*.

Minaj's wigs and unique costumes have made her a style icon to her fans.

CHAPTER 8

I Want to Be a Mogul

|||||||||||||||||||||||||||||||||||||||||||||||||||

Not one to slow down, Minaj immediately used the success of *Pink Friday* to propel herself into new business ventures. One week after the record's release, Minaj released the limited-edition Pink Friday 4 lipstick for MAC cosmetics. The lipstick was another success for Minaj, with stores selling out of the first batch the same day it was released.

The success of the MAC lipstick gave Minaj the confidence to set her big plans in motion. In interviews, Minaj began talking about her dream of becoming a one-woman mogul with an array of businesses under the Minaj brand. If her wide appeal among fans was any indication, this dream seemed entirely within her reach.

BARBS AND KENS

Minaj already had countless fans imitating her pink-wigged, over-the-top girlie style by dressing as "Barbs." These "super fans" are girls anywhere from eight years old to college aged attempting to look like Minaj, take on her vocal stylings, eat what she eats, and generally obsess over her. Minaj fully embraces her Barbs—especially the young female ones—and encourages them to experiment and to be anything they want.

> **"I say girls are beautiful and girls are sexy and they need to be told that."[1]**
>
> —NICKI MINAJ

Stylist Terence Davidson and a large group of assistants are in charge of handling Minaj's wigs, which practically have a life of their own. There are so many wigs that they require special packaging and vehicles to transport them during tours. Davidson and his team help create donut rolls, Marge Simpson hair, flipped styles, and more. Along with brightly colored and glittering accessories, the wig is key to Minaj's look. In one interview, Minaj joked with a reporter that she presses one button to make her hair grow and another for the color.

Not only women and young girls are fans of Minaj. She also has a vast following among young men, many of whom are homosexual. Maintaining the Barbie theme, these fans are referred to as "Kens" and wear short pink wigs.

While being gay has long been rather taboo in hip-hop, Minaj fully embraces homosexuality. She has opened a door for the gay community through her music and open-minded attitude. This has led some in the media to speculate on Minaj's own sexuality.

Like most topics in her career, when it comes to her sexuality, Minaj rejects labels, believing that "there are many shades in the middle, and you've got to let people feel comfortable with saying what they want to say when they want to say it."[2] Most of all, Minaj says she is interested in being her unique self.

|||||||||||||||||||||||||||||||||||||||||||||||||||||||||||||

SUPER BASS

Five weeks after its release, *Pink Friday* went platinum. In addition to "Roman's Revenge," "Check It Out," and "Moment 4 Life," there were three other singles on the record. These included "Did It On 'em," "Your Love," and "Fly," featuring pop sensation Rihanna. Like Minaj, Rihanna was born in the Caribbean, on the island of Barbados, and the two artists are close friends.

With seven singles out, the record company decided to release a deluxe version of *Pink Friday* that included three additional songs. One of them, "Super Bass," was an immediate hit, winning Best Hip-Hop Video on August 28 at the 2011 MTV VMAs. "Super Bass" became even more famous when eight-year-old Sophia Grace Brownlee from the United Kingdom was recorded singing it. The video, which went viral after being posted on the

Minaj has become close friends with singer Rihanna.

Minaj impersonator and YouTube sensation Sophia Grace Brownlee, *right*, attended the 2011 American Music Awards (AMAs) with her cousin Rosie, *left*.

video-sharing site YouTube, shows Sophia wearing a pink ballerina tutu while dancing and singing the song. Minaj met her miniature impersonator when she and Sophia appeared on the *Ellen DeGeneres Show* in October 2011.

BACK TO HER ROOTS

Minaj also celebrated her success by visiting her family in Trinidad and Tobago in 2010 just before the release of *Pink Friday*. During the visit, the usually costumed Minaj appeared more understated in jeans and a T-shirt with her hair pulled back and wearing almost no makeup.

The visit was special, particularly because it had been seven years since Minaj's last visit, when she had returned home for her grandmother's funeral. This time, the family came together under happier circumstances. To show her affection, Minaj took her family to a local shopping mall, letting them pick out whatever clothing or shoes they wanted.

Minaj wanted her family to "have whatever they want."[4]

While in Trinidad and Tobago, Minaj also performed for locals on the island of Saint James. On stage in her home turf, Minaj opened with "Monster" and the verse that made her famous. The audience cheered her on, roaring and jumping up and down. Afterward, the streets were filled with throngs of excited fans talking about her performance and begging her to return to Trinidad. For Minaj, performing for her own people was a "superb accomplishment."[5]

The trip was not just a great way to show love for the people of Trinidad and Tobago but also a tribute to the grandmother who had raised her

FAMILY TRAGEDY

In July 2011, Minaj and her family mourned the tragic death of her 27-year-old cousin, Nicholas Telemaque. Early in the morning, Telemaque was shot and killed close to his house in the East Flatbush neighborhood of Brooklyn, New York. Minaj took her grief to Twitter, where she posted photos of her cousin, whom she called "my precious."[6] Though he was killed in a somewhat rough and poor neighborhood, he was not said to be involved in gang activity. The police deemed the murder accidental.

until she was five years old. Minaj knew she would have made her grandmother proud. After all, she had accomplished a great deal by the time she was 28 years old. She had recorded what would become a platinum-selling album, set *Billboard* records, and became the most important woman in hip-hop in the 2010s.

|||||||||||

Minaj performed at the Super Bowl halftime show with Madonna and M.I.A.

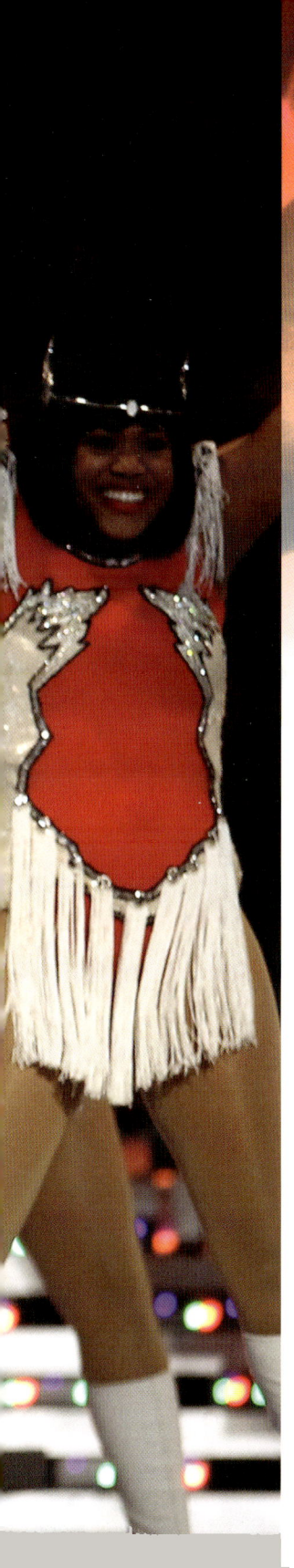

CHAPTER 9

Dreams Come True

||||||||||||||||||||||||||||||||||||||||||||||||||||||||

Super Bowl XLVI, between the New York Giants and the New England Patriots, was held on February 5, 2012, at Lucas Oil Stadium in Indianapolis, Indiana. Fans across the United States tuned in for the halftime show—one of the night's main events. The performance featured legendary pop singer Madonna. At 54 years old and with a career spanning more than 30 years, Madonna is among the top-selling female artists of all time. Everyone wanted to see what this known risk-taker would bring to her first-ever Super Bowl performance.

The set was extravagant. Madonna was unveiled to massive applause by dancers dressed as Greek warriors. Madonna started off the performance with her hit song "Vogue," then launched into a medley of songs with a group of dancers assembled around her in cheerleader uniforms. They began chanting "L-U-V Madonna! Y-O-U you wanna!" The camera zoomed in on one cheerleader resembling a modern-day Cleopatra, smiling in a blond wig and ornamented headband. The

M.I.A.

At the Super Bowl, Madonna and Minaj shared the stage with eclectic dance, electronic, and rap musician M.I.A. during the performance of "Give Me All Your Luvin'." The British performer was born Maya Arulpragasam on July 18, 1975, in London, England, but spent much of her childhood in the island country of Sri Lanka. Like Minaj, M.I.A. can be controversial and pushes boundaries musically while maintaining mass appeal. M.I.A. experienced the violence of civil war while growing up in Sri Lanka, causing her family to flee and return to London. She serves as an activist for humanitarian causes through her songwriting and public causes.

audience began cheering when they realized who they were looking at—hip-hop sensation Minaj.

Along with electronic pop-rap musician M.I.A., Minaj playfully danced to the beat in cheerleader fashion while pumping golden pom-poms in the air. Madonna glided through the beginning verses of her song "Give Me All Your Luvin'." Then Minaj launched into her solo, singing in her signature rough rap style with tongue-twisting lyrics.

As the song continued, Minaj shimmied against Madonna. For a moment they were equals. Side by side, it was easy to imagine that Minaj could one day take Madonna's place as a powerful female performer.

NUMBER 1 . . . AGAIN

Shortly after her Super Bowl performance, Minaj geared up for the release of her second studio album *Pink Friday . . . Roman Reloaded*. As the title suggested, Minaj planned to feature Roman Zolanski even more prominently on the new record, along with other characters. To market the record, singles were leaked one by one leading up to the full album release on April 3, 2012.

The album's first single, "Starships," debuted on February 14, 2012, just two days after Minaj's performance at the 2012 Grammy Awards on February 12. The song received mixed reviews initially, perhaps because its sound was more poppy than Minaj's rap-heavy signature tunes. Also contributing to the negative reception was Minaj's controversial performance at the Grammy Awards, which offended some viewers. During the performance of her song "Roman Holiday," Minaj enacted an exorcism on the stage, which was decorated to look like a Roman cathedral. Performing as if she were under the devilish spell of her alter ego, Roman, Minaj spoke in tongues and appeared to rise from the stage.

The pop sound of "Starships" combined with Minaj's controversial Grammy performance caused some critics to claim she was appealing to the mainstream by being more like singer and performer Lady Gaga. The *Los Angeles Times'* Gerrick D. Kennedy wrote:

Minaj's 2012 Grammy performance was controversial.

Minaj should brace herself for Lady Gaga copycat claims. When she hit the scene, critics quickly slugged her as "rap's Lady Gaga" because of the wigs and kooky outfits, but Minaj proved herself the minute she opened her mouth—whether it was on her own single or stealing the spotlight from someone else.[1]

COMPARISONS TO GAGA

Minaj has often been called "hip-hop's Gaga" because similar to Lady Gaga, she has an over-the-top, eclectic style and a tendency to push the envelope toward the avant-garde. Both performers come from a highly theatrical background, and Lady Gaga reached mass fame shortly before Minaj. Gaga earned eight awards at the same VMA show where Minaj had her first breakout performance in 2010. Minaj's enactment of an exorcism at the 2012 Grammys begged comparisons to Gaga, who created her own cathedral scene during her performance at the 2009 VMAs. Gaga was also the MAC Viva Glam spokesperson before Minaj took on the role in 2012.

Minaj, however, hit back at the claims during an April 2012 interview with ABC's *Nightline*. Wearing wigs and over-the-top costumes doesn't mean she's trying to be like Lady Gaga, Minaj said. "Gaga is a fantastic artist. She's paved her way. She's opened her own lane. But I feel like I have my own lane. And we never cross, ever!" she said.[2]

"Starships" quickly became a hit single, and its music video won Minaj the MTV VMA for Best Female Video on September 6, 2012. It was still on the *Billboard* Top 10 in May 2012, a month after the full album's release. The album includes rap-heavy songs, something Minaj's fans from her mixtape days could appreciate. The song "Beez in the Trap" featured rapper 2 Chainz, who Minaj knew from her days in Atlanta.

Early critiques of *Pink Friday . . . Roman Reloaded* were quickly overshadowed by the album's rapid success. It debuted at Number 1 and maintained its spot in the Top 10 well after its release. Notably, its success unseated Madonna's album *MDNA*, which dropped from Number 1 to Number 8 after its first week on the *Billboard* chart. Just a few months before, Minaj had felt honored when she performed with Madonna at the Super Bowl. Now Minaj's record was outperforming Madonna's. Could this mean Minaj was on her way to surpassing the Queen of Pop?

FASHIONISTA FOREVER

Minaj has been vocal about her plans to extend her brand beyond music. In addition to her fashion and cosmetics lines, she has an interest in returning to acting and writing an autobiography. In July 2012, she even lent her voice to Steffie, the ladybug in the film *Ice Age: Continental Drift*.

Before her Grammy and Super Bowl performances, Minaj once again made headlines during New York City Fashion Week in September 2011. At the Carolina Herrera and Oscar de la Renta runway shows, Minaj accompanied legendary *Vogue* editor in chief Anna Wintour. Although she was in the company of fashion royalty, Minaj chose to wear something edgy. Among her clothing items during Fashion Week were a multicolored felt gumball dress, a donut roll wig, and tiger stripes on her fur hat and face.

Minaj's entry into the fashion world didn't stop there. In November 2011, she helped launch the Versace for H&M line. Alongside singer Prince, Minaj performed at the event wearing a jewel-covered jacket custom designed by Donatella Versace.

In December 2011, Minaj received one of her most exciting honors in fashion. Mattel produced a one-of-a kind Nicki Minaj Barbie Doll. The doll resembled the star with almond-shaped eyes and her signature pink wig with bangs. It wore a white, rhinestone-encrusted bustier and belt. For Minaj, a lifetime lover of Barbie, this was a "very major moment."[3] All proceeds from the auction

Minaj showed off her style when she accompanied Anna Wintour, *right*, to New York City Fashion Week in 2011.

of the Minaj doll went to Project Angel Food, a nonprofit organization that helps feed Acquired Immune Deficiency Syndrome (AIDS) and Human immunodeficiency virus (HIV) sufferers.

Minaj is also the 2012 MAC Viva Glam spokesperson and is already developing a top-selling nail polish line with nail products manufacturer OPI. In the future, she plans to launch her own clothing line. Following

Minaj continues broadening her résumé and star power.

her own daring style, she intends to keep her "runway Harajuku" line cutting-edge rather than mainstream.

AMERICAN IDOL JUDGE

After much speculation, on September 16, 2012, Minaj was officially announced as the newest judge on the Fox television network singing competition *American Idol*. Minaj's deal with the show was worth $12 million. Mike Darnell, Fox's president of alternative programming, said of Minaj, "Nicki's an unbelievably captivating international phenomenon who has made an indelible mark on rap and pop."[4] Singers Keith Urban and Mariah Carey also joined Minaj as new judges for the show's twelfth season.

Critics said Minaj helps *American Idol* represent the hip-hop genre as a judge and also draws viewers from her young fan base. Minaj said she had been a fan of *American Idol*, which was why she decided to join the show. "I remember watching 'American Idol' in the first season and feeling inspired," Minaj said.[5]

As Minaj's star power continues to increase, her mother offered some advice to her daughter: "Keep standing. No matter what life throws at you, dance."[6] Minaj appears to be doing exactly that.

||||||||||

TIMELINE

1982

Onika Tanya Maraj is born in Saint James, Port of Spain, Trinidad and Tobago, on December 8.

1988

Minaj relocates to Queens, New York.

1997

Minaj is accepted to LaGuardia Arts High School.

2007

Lil Wayne discovers Minaj through *The Come Up* DVD series. She is featured on his *Da Drought 3* mixtape.

2009

Minaj's *Beam Me Up, Scotty* mixtape is released in April.

2009

Minaj is officially signed to Young Money Entertainment as its first female member with a 360 record deal in August.

2001

Minaj appears in the off-off-Broadway production *In Case You Forget*.

2002

Minaj joins the Hoodstars, a New York City rap group.

2006

Music producer Fendi discovers Minaj through her MySpace page.

2010

Minaj's single with Mariah Carey, "Up Out My Face," is released in February.

2010

The music video for "My Chick Bad," with Minaj dressed as Freddy Krueger, premiers on BET on February 19.

2010

The hit song "Bedrock" by Young Money crew is released on March 22.

TIMELINE

2010

Minaj receives critical acclaim for her verse on Kanye West's single "Monster" upon its release in September.

2010

On October 8, Minaj sets the *Billboard* record for being the solo female artist with the most singles on the Hot 100 chart at once.

2010

On September 12, Minaj performs at the 2010 MTV VMAs with will.i.am.

2011

Minaj wins Best Hip-Hop Video for "Super Bass" at the MTV VMAs on August 28.

2012

Minaj performs with Madonna and M.I.A. at Super Bowl XLVI on February 5.

2012

Minaj performs at the Grammy Awards on February 12.

2010

On November 23, Minaj's first solo record *Pink Friday* is released along with limited edition Pink Friday lipstick by MAC.

2011

In October, Minaj appears on the *Ellen DeGeneres Show* with 8-year-old fan and YouTube sensation Sophia Grace Brownlee.

2011

Minaj wins Favorite Hip-Hop Artist and Album at the American Music Awards on November 21.

2012

Minaj's second solo album *Pink Friday . . . Roman Reloaded* debuts at Number 1 on the *Billboard* chart on April 3.

2012

Minaj wins Best Female Video for "Starships" at the VMAs on September 6.

2012

In September, Minaj is announced as a judge on the twelfth season of *American Idol*.

GET THE SCOOP

FULL NAME

Onika Tanya Maraj

DATE OF BIRTH

December 8, 1982

PLACE OF BIRTH

St. James, Port of Spain, Trinidad and Tobago

SELECTED ALBUMS

Pink Friday (2010); *Pink Friday…Roman Reloaded* (2012)

SELECTED FILMS AND TELEVISION APPEARANCES

Ice Age: Continental Drift (2012), *American Idol* (began filming in 2012)

SELECTED AWARDS

- Won 2010 BET Award for Best Female Hip-Hop Artist
- Won 2010 BET Award for Best New Artist
- Won 2011 American Music Award for Best Rap/ Hip-Hop Artist
- Won 2011 American Music Award for Best Rap/ Hip-Hop Album

- Won 2011 MTV Video Music Award for Best Hip-Hop Video
- Won 2012 MTV Video Music Award for Best Female Video
- Nominated for 2012 Grammy Awards for Best Rap Album, Best Rap Performance, and Best New Artist

PHILANTHROPY

In December 2011, Mattel Inc. auctioned off Minaj's one-of-a-kind Barbie doll with proceeds going to Project Angel Food, a nonprofit that helps feed HIV and AIDS sufferers. Minaj teamed up with singer Ricky Martin and MAC Cosmetics to spread HIV and AIDS awareness in Latin America.

> "I like playing dress up. When I do my voices and faces, I don't think about anything. My mind stops."
>
> —*NICKI MINAJ*

GLOSSARY

adversity—An instance or condition of serious or continued misfortune.

animalistic—Of, relating to, or resembling an animal or animals.

avant-garde—New or experimental concepts in the arts.

Billboard—A music chart system used by the music recording industry to measure record popularity or sales.

collaborate—To work together in order to create or produce a work, such as a song or an album.

debut—A first appearance.

demo—An initial recording meant to demonstrate a musician's talent to a record producer.

freestyle—To perform verses on the spot rather than using prewritten lyrics.

hip-hop—A style of popular music associated with US urban culture that features rap spoken against a background of electronic music or beats.

iconography—Symbolic representation, especially the conventional meanings attached to an image.

legendary—Someone or something well-known or famous.

mentor—A person with experience in a specific field who guides someone with less experience.

mogul—Someone who has achieved tremendous wealth.

persona—A popular hip-hop device in which the rapper takes on a voice and personality that isn't actually his or her own.

platinum—A certification by the Recording Industry Association of America that an album has sold more than a million copies. Multiplatinum indicates that the album has sold more than 2 million copies.

precedent—An example or instance used to justify later similar occurrences.

reminiscent—Awakening memories of something similar.

single—An individual song that is distributed on its own over the radio and other mediums.

speculate—To ponder or reflect on a subject.

ADDITIONAL RESOURCES

SELECTED BIBLIOGRAPHY

Ganz, Caryn. "The Curious Case of Nicki Minaj." *Out*. Out
Magazine, 12 Sept. 2010. Web. 15 Apr. 2012.

Newman, Judith. "Just Try to Look Away." *Allure* Apr. 2012:
236. Print.

"Nicki Minaj." Narr. Beng Spies. *E! True Hollywood Story*.
NBC Universal, New York City. 13 July 2011. Television.

Nicki Minaj: My Time Now. Dir. Michael John Warren.
Radical Media and MTV Networks, 2010. Television.

Yaeger, Lynn. "True Colors: Nicki Minaj." *Vogue*. Vogue,
21 Feb. 2012. Web. 9 July 2012.

FURTHER READINGS

Bynoe, Yvonne. *Encyclopedia of Rap and Hip Hop Culture*.
Connecticut: Greenwood, 2008.

Cornish, Melanie. *The History of Hip Hop*. New York:
Crabtree Publishing Company, 2009.

WEB SITES

To learn more about Nicki Minaj, visit ABDO Publishing
Company online at **www.abdopublishing.com**. Web sites
about Nicki Minaj are featured on our Book Links page.
These links are routinely monitored and updated to provide
the most current information available.

PLACES TO VISIT

The Grammy Museum

800 W. Olympic Boulevard, Los Angeles, CA 90015-1300
213-765-6800
www.grammymuseum.org
The Grammy Museum features exhibits related to many genres of music.

LaGuardia Arts

100 Amsterdam Avenue, New York, New York 10023
212-496-0700
www.laguardiahs.org
Minaj attended the high school that inspired the 1980 film *Fame*. The school offers several student events during the school year, including art exhibits and theater, musical, and dance performances.

SOURCE NOTES

CHAPTER 1. A RISING STAR

1. *Nicki Minaj: My Time Now*. Dir. Michael John Warren. Radical Media and MTV Networks, 2010. Television.

CHAPTER 2. LITTLE GIRL IN THE BIG APPLE

1. "Nicki Minaj." Narr. Beng Spies. *E! True Hollywood Story*. NBC Universal, New York City. 13 July 2011. Television.

2. Ibid.

3. Ibid.

4. Ibid.

5. Siobhan O'Connor. "Character Study: Just How Real Is Nicki Minaj?" *Vibe*. Vibe, 23 June 2010. Web. 4 Apr. 2012.

6. Judith Newman. "Just Try to Look Away." *Allure* Apr. 2012: 236. Print.

7. Caryn Ganz. "*The Curious Case of Nicki Minaj*." *Out*. Out Magazine, 12 Sept. 2010. Web. 15 Apr. 2012.

8. Rob Markman. "Nicki Minaj Encourages Barbs Not To Be Afraid To 'Experiment.'" *MTV*. MTV, 2 Apr. 2012. Web. 10 Apr. 2012.

CHAPTER 3. I'M AN ACTOR!

1. *Nicki Minaj: My Time Now*. Dir. Michael John Warren. Radical Media and MTV Networks, 2010. Television.

2. Ibid.

3. Siobhan O'Connor. "Character Study: Just How Real Is Nicki Minaj?" *Vibe*. Vibe, 23 June 2010. Web. 4 Apr. 2012.

4. Newman, Judith. "Just Try to Look Away." *Allure* Apr. 2012: 236. Print.

5. "Nicki Minaj." Narr. Beng Spies. *E! True Hollywood Story*. NBC Universal, New York City. 13 July 2011. Television.

6. Ibid.

7. Ibid.

8. Ibid.

CHAPTER 4. ONE DAY YOU'LL KNOW WHO NICKI MINAJ IS

1. "Nicki Minaj." Narr. Beng Spies. *E! True Hollywood Story*. NBC Universal, New York City. 13 July 2011. Television.

2. Ibid.

3. Ibid.

4. Siobhan O'Connor. "Character Study: Just How Real Is Nicki Minaj?" *Vibe*. Vibe, 23 June 2010. Web. 4 Apr. 2012.

5. "Nicki Minaj." Narr. Beng Spies. *E! True Hollywood Story*. NBC Universal, New York City. 13 July 2011. Television.

6. Jon Caramanica. "Gucci Mane, No Holds Barred." *New York Times*. New York Times, 11 Dec. 2009. Web. 1 May 2012.

CHAPTER 5. A WOMAN'S TURN

1. Miss Info. "Nicki Minaj: Self-Possessed." *Complex Music*. Complex Media, 20 Mar. 2012. Web. 9 July 2012.

2. Nadeska Alexis. "Nicki Minaj Channels Barbie In 'Playtime Is Over' Mixtape Shoot." *MTV*. MTV, 4 Apr. 2012. Web. 15 Apr. 2012.

3. D. L. Chandler. "Lil' Kim Video Calls Nicki Minaj A 'Carbon Copy.'" *MTV News*. MTV, 1 Mar. 2011. Web. 6 Aug. 2012.

4. Mariel Concepcion. "Nicki Minaj Says Lil Kim Will Be Remembered As 'Sore Loser.'" *Billboard*. Billboard, 22 Nov. 2010. Web. 6 Aug. 2012.

5. *Nicki Minaj: My Time Now*. Dir. Michael John Warren. Radical Media and MTV Networks, 2010. Television.

6. Nina Chantele. "Nicki Minaj Mobbed in London." *WGCI-FM*. Clear Channel Media and Entertainment, 20 Jan. 2011. Web. 6 Aug. 2012.

7. "Nicki Minaj." Narr. Beng Spies. *E! True Hollywood Story*. NBC Universal, New York City. 13 July 2011. Television.

8. Ibid.

9. Ibid.

CHAPTER 6. THE "IT" GIRL OF HIP-HOP

1. Miss Info. "Nicki Minaj: Self-Possessed." *Complex Music*. Complex Media, 20 Mar. 2012. Web. 9 July 2012.

2. Lynn Yaeger. "True Colors: Nicki Minaj." *Vogue*. Vogue, 21 Feb. 2012. Web. 9 July 2012.

3. Siobhan O'Connor. "Character Study: Just How Real Is Nicki Minaj?" *Vibe*. Vibe, 23 June 2010. Web. 4 Apr. 2012.

4. Miss Info. "Nicki Minaj: Self-Possessed." *Complex Music*. Complex Media, 20 Mar. 2012. Web. 9 July 2012.

5. Shaheem Reid. "Ross Says 'Monster' Proves Nicki Minaj Is 'One of The Greatest.'" *MTV*. MTV, 28 Sept. 2011. Web. 15 Apr. 2012.

6. Ibid.

CHAPTER 7. WHO IS NICKI MINAJ?

1. "Nicki Minaj." Narr. Beng Spies. *E! True Hollywood Story*. NBC Universal, New York City. 13 July 2011. Television.

2. Jorge Rivas. "Nicki Minaj Gets Personal on Childhood Abuse." *ColorLines-News for Action*. Applied Research Center, 2011. Web. 15 Apr. 2012.

3. Miss Info. "Nicki Minaj: Self-Possessed." *Complex Music*. Complex Media, 20 Mar. 2012. Web. 9 July 2012.

4. Caryn Ganz. "*The Curious Case of Nicki Minaj*." Out. Out Magazine, 12 Sept. 2010. Web. 15 Apr. 2012.

5. *Nicki Minaj: My Time Now*. Dir. Michael John Warren. Radical Media and MTV Networks, 2010. Television.

6. Lynn Yaeger. "True Colors: Nicki Minaj." *Vogue*. Vogue, 21 Feb. 2012. Web. 9 July 2012.

7. "Nicki Minaj." Narr. Beng Spies. *E! True Hollywood Story*. NBC Universal, New York City. 13 July 2011. Television.

8. Caryn Ganz. "*The Curious Case of Nicki Minaj*." Out. Out Magazine, 12 Sept. 2010. Web. 15 Apr. 2012.

9. *Nicki Minaj: My Time Now*. Dir. Michael John Warren. Radical Media and MTV Networks, 2010. Television.

10. Owen Stretch. "Nicki Minaj - Roman's Revenge Lyrics."*MetroLyrics*. MetroLyrics, n.d. Web. 12 July 2012.

CHAPTER 8. I WANT TO BE A MOGUL

1. Judith Newman. "Just Try to Look Away." *Allure* Apr. 2012: 236. Print.

2. Caryn Ganz. *"The Curious Case of Nicki Minaj."* *Out.* Out Magazine, 12 Sept. 2010. Web. 15 Apr. 2012.

3. Judith Newman. "Just Try to Look Away." *Allure* Apr. 2012: 236. Print.

4. *Nicki Minaj: My Time Now.* Dir. Michael John Warren. Radical Media and MTV Networks, 2010. Television.

5. Ibid.

6. Rob Markman. "Nicki Minaj Mourns Cousin Nicholas Telemaque's Death." *MTV*. MTV, 5 Jul. 2011. Web. 12 July 2012.

CHAPTER 9. DREAMS COME TRUE

1. Gerrick D. Kennedy. "Nicki Minaj's Starships Reaffirms Her Pop Star Aims." *Los Angeles Times*. Los Angeles Times, 14 Feb. 2012. Web. 9 July 2012.

2. Lauren Effron and Erin Brady. "Nicki Minaj: 6 Surprising Revelations, Including Her Thoughts on Lady Gaga." *ABC News*. ABC News, 9 Apr. 2012. Web. 9 July 2012.

3. Shauna Wright. "Nicki Minaj Fights AIDS and HIV—In Barbie Form." *The FW*. The FW, 5 Dec. 2011. Web. 25 Apr. 2012.

4. James Hibberd. "'American Idol' Announces Judges: Keith Urban, Nicki Minaj Confirmed." *Entertainment Weekly*. Entertainment Weekly, 16 Sept. 2012. Web. 18 Sept. 2012.

5. Gil Kaufman. "Nicki Minaj Says She Answered Call For 'American Idol' Gig As A 'Fan.'" *MTV News*. MTV, 18 Sept. 2012. Web. 18 Sept. 2012.

6. "Nicki Minaj." Narr. Beng Spies. *E! True Hollywood Story*. NBC Universal, New York City. 13 July 2011. Television.

INDEX

ABOUT THE AUTHOR

Ashley Rae Harris lives in Chicago, Illinois. She has authored several books for adolescents, including *Tupac Shakur: Multi-Platinum Rapper*, *Arms Trade*, and titles in the *Essential Health: Strong, Beautiful Girls* series. Her work has appeared in *Time Out Chicago* and *Venuszine*. She holds a master's degree from the University of Chicago.

PHOTO CREDITS